The Little Book of Daily Rituals

*Simple Self-Care Routines to Refresh
Your Mind, Body and Spirit*

THE LITTLE BOOK OF DAILY RITUALS

An Hachette UK Company
www.hachette.co.uk

Vie Books, an imprint of Summersdale Publishers Ltd
Part of Octopus Publishing Group Limited
Carmelite House
50 Victoria Embankment
LONDON
EC4Y 0DZ
UK

Hachette Ireland
8 Castlecourt
Castleknock
Dublin 15
Ireland

www.summersdale.com

www.hachettebooksireland.ie

Printed and bound in China

ISBN: 978-1-78783-224-4

Substantial discounts on bulk quantities of Summersdale books are available to corporations, professional associations and other organizations. For details contact general enquiries: telephone: +44 (0) 1243 771107 or email: enquiries@summersdale.com.

The Little Book
of Daily Rituals

*Simple Self-Care Routines to Refresh
Your Mind, Body and Spirit*

Vicki Vrint

The little things?
The little moments?
They aren't little.

Jon Kabat-Zinn

CONTENTS

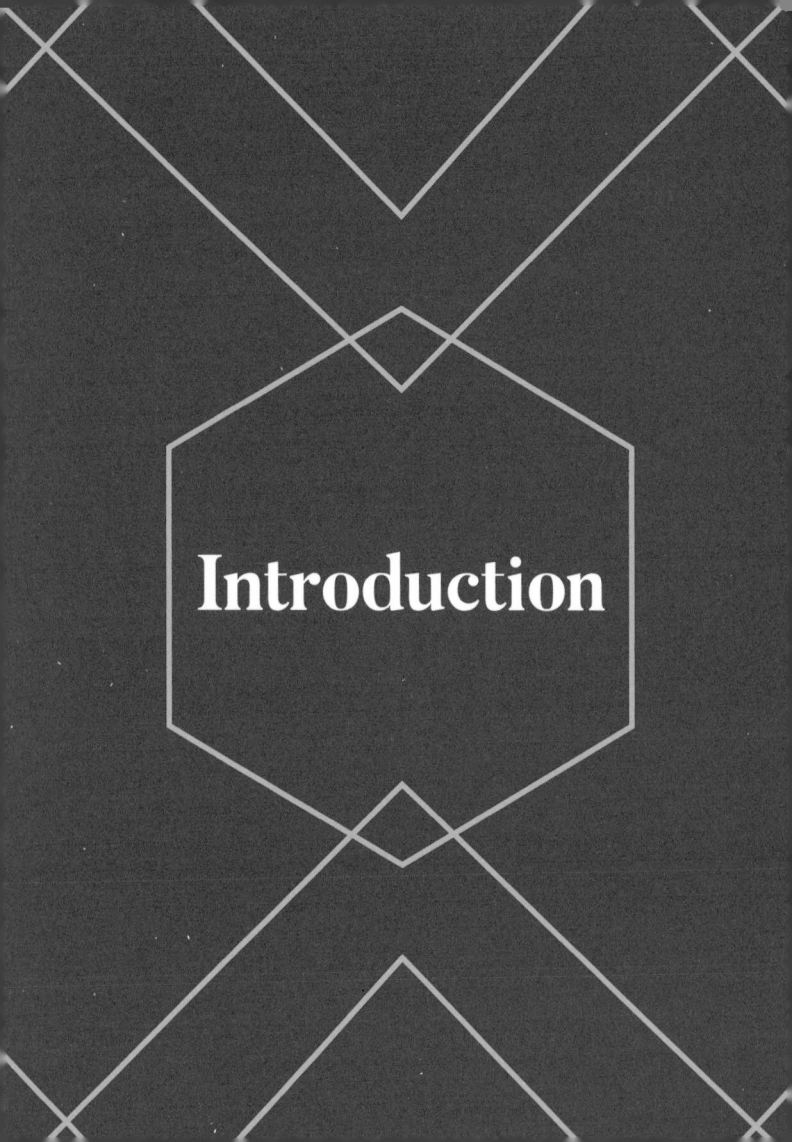

Introduction

Rituals are activities we carry out mindfully and with reverence. They give us an opportunity to slow down and get in touch with our thoughts and feelings. You can use them to reflect on what you want to achieve, to motivate you to take action or to help you face the challenges of day-to-day life.

Numerous studies have shown how important it is to take time out for ourselves every day – and how not doing so can lead to stress, depression and health issues such as high blood pressure and depleted immunity – but it can be difficult to do this in practice. Carrying out a regular ritual, such as a meditation or some simple breathing exercises, is an easy and rewarding way to include an element of self-care in your day.

This book includes over eighty such rituals to refresh your mind, body and spirit. Whether you want to create time for self-care, to find inspiration or to slow down and connect with the world around you, there is a ritual in this book to help you.

How do rituals work?

Rituals offer you mindful moments to savour during the day; moments to help you pause, focus on your intentions and reflect on what matters to you. Whether you use them to celebrate everyday wonders or to remind yourself to indulge in a little self-care, they will always be peaceful and positive experiences. Repeating a ritual regularly means that your mind recognizes it as a cue to relax into the exercise, so the more you practise the better the results will be.

Some of the rituals in this book list items you might like to use, but these are just suggestions. (Your rituals will be most effective if they are meaningful to you, so feel free to personalize them.) What matters most is that you pause and give all your attention to what you're doing – it's concentrating on your intentions in this way that leads to positive results.

Have fun exploring and experiencing the life-enhancing power of rituals!

Mind

A simple meditation

Intention: To still the mind and experience a moment of calm.

The benefits of meditation are so wide-reaching that practising this simple ritual regularly – perhaps as part of your evening routine – will have a positive impact on everything, from your physical and mental well-being to your energy levels and quality of sleep. You don't really need any equipment to do it, but you might like to burn some incense or diffuse some oil to help you relax (lavender or ylang ylang are both good for this).

Find somewhere quiet and comfortable to meditate, lying down or sitting, whichever suits you. There's no need to close your eyes at first; just take a moment to settle. Listen to the sounds around you and become aware of how your body feels, noticing your points of contact with the surface beneath you.

Focus on your breathing – slowly in through the nose and out through the mouth – and allow your eyes to close. Continue to focus on your breathing, counting "one" for each in-breath and "two" for each out-breath, slowly and steadily.

Your thoughts will wander, and that is perfectly fine. It's natural for the mind to want to do so. Meditating isn't about silencing your thoughts, it's about distancing yourself from them: watching them come, and then letting them go as you realize your mind has wandered, and refocusing on your breathing. When you are ready to finish, expand your bubble of awareness; listen to the sounds around you, feel the surface beneath you, and then open your eyes.

A song-a-day ritual

Intention: To use music to nurture your mind, body and spirit.

Tapping in to the mood-boosting, stress-busting power of music every day is one of the easiest and most uplifting rituals you can undertake. Whatever your mood there will be a song to lighten your heart, to make you smile or to comfort you while you cry… and chances are that you already know what that song is.

Make a point of listening to a song every day, whenever you need it most. You could choose an upbeat tune you loved at high school to energize you when you first wake up; or – if you're having a difficult time – listen to your "soul song", the one whose lyrics have always seemed to echo your own experiences. Or how about ending your working day with a celebratory dance around the kitchen to whatever's trending on your music app?

A pilgrimage ritual

Intention: To visit somewhere awe-inspiring and feel wonder.

For some of us it will be the beauty of the landscape or the spectacle of the night sky, for others it might be a breathtaking piece of architecture or a place of worship. Whatever it is that inspires awe in you, make time to visit it regularly. Research has shown that seeing and reacting to extraordinary sights boosts the immune system and positively affects our behaviour. We benefit on a spiritual level, too, as these experiences of wonder remind us of our place in a world that is much bigger than ourselves.

You'll know what type of destination appeals to you, but don't feel you have to go too far afield. The wonders of a natural landscape are never far away and you may discover an awe-inspiring site on your doorstep. Visit it, experience the details and reflect on what makes it so special to you. Repeat as necessary.

A ritual for self-expression

Intention: To free your unexpressed words and emotions.

Bottling up your feelings can lead to frustration, stress and even physical symptoms, as well as damaging your concentration and overall happiness. In some situations, it may not be appropriate (or possible) to voice your feelings directly, or you may simply have general worries you need to release to maintain your peace of mind. This ritual will help you to set these unspoken thoughts free.

You could use:

- ◆ Peppermint essential oil and a burner
- ◆ Peppermint tea
- ◆ Slips of paper and a pen
- ◆ A heatproof bowl and matches

Diffuse some drops of peppermint oil in a burner and breathe slowly and deeply for a few moments, focusing on your breath and the aroma of the oil. (You can also sip peppermint tea – peppermint relaxes the throat, the point of self-expression.) Release any tension in your jaw and shoulders, and feel your throat muscles relaxing.

When you're ready to begin, ask yourself how you're feeling and say aloud any answers that come to mind, such as "I'm feeling upset," or, "the way that I was treated at work was unfair." Don't hold back. Carry on speaking, airing any tensions or worries that come to mind.

When you've expressed everything you need to, take the pen and paper and write down any words that sum up what you've said, such as "anger" or "sadness". Burn them in the heatproof bowl and sense your worries disappearing as you do so. Repeat the ritual whenever you feel the tension of unexpressed feelings returning.

A decluttering ritual

Intention: To reap the mental, physical and spiritual rewards of a declutter.

Clutter adds to our stress levels and makes it hard for us to enjoy any time we've set aside for relaxation. If decluttering sounds more like a chore than a self-care ritual, remember that it's therapeutic and an excellent exercise in mindfulness. Find a regular five-minute slot in your day and use this to tackle whichever area is most cluttered. You could target a kitchen cupboard, your work desk or even just turn out your make-up bag or wallet.

Add a mindful element to your decluttering by focusing on the task at hand and concentrating on the textures and details of the items you're handling. Once your area is clear, wipe it down with this home-made witch hazel cleaner, which has natural anti-bacterial properties.

Mix ¼ cup of witch hazel disinfectant with ½ cup of water and around 8 drops of peppermint or tea-tree essential oil. Pour into a spray bottle and use to bring some sparkle to your newly cleared area.

If it's been messy for a while, you could also add a spiritual element to your decluttering by cleansing the energy of the area you've just cleaned. You can do this by smudging (see p.84), clapping your hands or ringing a bell to dispel negative or stale energy.

A candle ritual

Intention: To focus your mind
and find peace when you need it.

If you're new to meditation or spiritual practice, this candle ritual is a lovely place to start. All you need is a candle and somewhere quiet and comfortable to sit for a while. (It's a nice meditation to perform at the end of the day, before bed.) Practise regularly and you'll find it easier to still your mind – a useful skill to take back with you into the rush of day-to-day life.

Turn off any bright lights or distractions and light your candle. Sit in front of it and stare steadily at the flame, refocusing whenever you find yourself distracted by everyday thoughts. Now, hold the image of the candle in your mind and close your eyes for a few seconds. Open your eyes to refresh the image. Practise this for five minutes, closing your eyes for a little longer each time. Carry this ritual out often and you'll be able to visualize the candle and meditate when you need to, wherever you are.

A just-say-hello ritual

Intention: To meet and greet someone new.

In order for us to stay happy, it's important to maintain connections with other people. Talking to others not only boosts our mood, it also helps us to develop a strong sense of identity. Just spending five minutes chatting to someone can help us to feel more positive – and by making time for regular conversations with others you'll be boosting their spirits, too.

Make a resolution to say hello to someone as often as you can. Most people enjoy talking about their experiences and some of the most inspirational stories come from the people we meet face to face. Try chatting to people the next time you're in a queue, at the bus stop, or paying for your shopping. If you're feeling shy, you can always start a conversation with a compliment. Make your just-say-hello ritual an attentive one: ask questions, be open-minded and you'll both enjoy the experience.

A ritual for setting boundaries

Intention: To set healthy boundaries and protect yourself from unwanted burdens.

We are often taught to put others before ourselves and can end up saying yes to requests when we would like to say no. Learning to set strong boundaries will help you to live in a more authentic way and to say your "yeses" wholeheartedly.

This visualization is straightforward but very beneficial. It helps you to maintain your priorities (and calm) when you go out into the world, and to come back without taking on more responsibilities than you want to or picking up negative energy from others.

You could use:

- A smooth pebble
- Some red paint or a red marker pen
- Cedarwood essential oil, for strength and focus

Diffuse a few drops of cedarwood oil, or dab them (diluted according to the label) onto your pressure points (your wrists, your temples or just behind your ears). Focus on breathing in the scent and sit quietly for a moment.

Setting boundaries is all about staying calm, being firm and knowing your own mind. Think about this and pick a power word that encompasses these things for you: "respect", "strength" or "authenticity", perhaps. Meditate on it for a moment or two.

Now write that word on your stone (or draw a suitable rune or symbol to represent it). Sit and hold the stone, visualizing the energy of your power word flowing from the stone and into yourself. Let this energy expand around you, forming a shield or bubble of gold light. You will feel safe and protected inside it. Focus on this shield when you find yourself in any boundary-challenging encounters during the day and centre yourself within it before you make any decisions.

You can take your stone with you when you go out and about on challenging days – or simply keep it in mind – and use this meditation to strengthen your boundaries whenever you need to.

A forest-bathing ritual

Intention: To relax in the
company of trees.

Being outside in nature has a powerful, positive effect on our well-being. We've all experienced how a walk in the wild can both calm and invigorate us. Forest bathing – spending time mindfully among trees – is particularly beneficial.

To forest bathe, use your senses to engage with the environment. Feel the bark of the trees; listen to birdsong and gaze at the sunlight on the leaves above. Go macro and focus on the smallest details: unfurling buds or the colours of a beetle's carapace. Have a favourite tree that you visit regularly and watch it change throughout the year. Sit beneath it, with its trunk at your back and soak up its wonderful energy.

Make a ritual of spending time with trees as often as you can. If you don't live near a wood, don't despair; spending time in a park or local garden can be just as effective.

A ritual for tuning in to your intuition

Intention: To tune in to the energy around you and recognize your response to it.

We have an energetic connection with many things in our lives – from the familiar items in our homes to the people we meet every day – and many of these encounters give us good vibes. This ritual is a lovely mindfulness exercise on its own, but it will also teach you how to be more aware of these connections, to spot them elsewhere and to deepen your understanding of your spiritual self.

Simply spend ten minutes holding one of your treasured objects; it could be a favourite book, your coffee mug or an item of jewellery. Focus on it, taking in all its details, feeling the weight of it in your hand and savouring the feelings it evokes. Repeat this whenever you can. The ritual will help you to pause during your day and to become more in tune with your gut reaction to new experiences in the future, too.

An it's-an-emergency-I'm-really-ANGRY! ritual

Intention: To learn – in times of anger – to release, record, reflect and react.

We all get angry at times: anger is a natural reaction to the frustrations and injustices – big and small – of everyday life, but how we deal with that initial burst of feeling can have a huge impact on our well-being and that of those around us, too. This little ritual is a good one to practise whenever big emotions strike, to make sure that your reactions are considered and calm, and that they represent you at your best... In other words, it's a ritual to stop you doing something you may regret!

1. Release

A Bad Thing has happened and you're in the initial stages of anger, so release some of that emotion in a controlled way. Rant to a friend (or yourself – best done somewhere private); put on a song with meaningful lyrics and sing along wholeheartedly; go for a run... There are plenty of things you can do to vent, which don't involve leaving angry voicemails!

2. Record

Once you've released a burst of emotion, find a little perspective by writing down exactly what happened. Now put this account away and do something else – something altruistic that involves spending time with other people is a good choice.

3. Reflect

After a day or so, look back on The Bad Thing in a calm way. Try picturing what happened from the view point of an observer so that you can see your own part in events. If you still feel your emotions rising at this point, picture the incident on a TV screen and "turn down" the sound as you review it. Reflect on how you feel.

4. React

You should now be in a good position to decide how best to react – whether that's with a calm message to someone involved or a note in your journal on what you would do differently in the future.

A ritual for a new beginning

Intention: To bring energy and excitement
to every new beginning.

Many of us love the feeling that a fresh start brings and embrace
this at New Year, putting all our efforts into a resolution or two.
But you don't need to restrict this bright energy and enthusiasm
to once every twelve months. Every day is a new beginning and
presents us with the opportunity to wipe the slate clean and start
afresh. In fact, you can begin each day with a new resolution if
you wish. You don't need to go for a biggie every time. A simple
affirmation when you wake up – "Today I will take everything in
my stride," for example – is an inspirational and positive way to
start the day.

On days when you're starting a new project (at work or at home) you might like to go a little further and make more of your ritual. Clear your work area of any traces of former projects and clean it with some witch hazel spray (see p.16). Once your space is fresh and clear, choose a picture, symbol or motto that represents your project and put this somewhere prominent to inspire you while you work.

You could also charge up a crystal or token to add some positive spiritual vibes to your project: a sodalite crystal charged up over an orange candle for creativity, for example, or a citrine stone charged over a green candle for prosperity. To do this, light the candle in your meditation space and meditate on it for a while, focusing on your project and the results you want to achieve. Now carefully pass the crystal over the candle flame three times to energize it. Keep the crystal in your workspace while you carry out your project.

A pause-after-work ritual

Intention: To make a meaningful transition between work and home mode.

If you rush straight into your home activities as soon as you get through the door after a hectic day at work, you can end up introducing a level of stress to your precious personal time that doesn't belong there at all. Make a ritual of pausing when you get in and letting your thoughts settle before you embrace the evening.

Unfurl a yoga mat and spend five minutes lying on it as soon as you get home. This may sound a little quirky, but lying down is (obviously) very grounding and calming, and the perfect antidote to a busy day. If you enjoy yoga, you could include a few gentle floor poses now – such as Butterfly or Happy Baby pose – but simply lying on your back and relaxing into the floor is enough to help you change down a gear after a busy day.

A ritual for
observing your emotions

Intention: To remind you that emotions come
and go, and to help you observe them.

Many of the rituals in this book give you a chance to pause
and experience your thoughts and feelings. Your emotions are
natural reactions to the events of your day, but it's important to
remember that they don't define who you are.

Practise this ritual when you're struggling with a low mood or
negative feelings. Sit quietly and focus on your physical body
and its point of contact with the earth. Once grounded, allow
your emotions to come and go; inhabit them for a moment but
don't get caught up with them. You could visualize each in a
bubble floating past or as a leaf floating along the surface of the
river. Watch the emotion come, allow yourself to experience it
fully and then let it drift off while you remain sitting calmly and
steadily in place. You may like to repeat the affirmation "This, too,
will pass."

A forgive-yourself ritual

Intention: To remind you to forgive yourself, because you are marvellous.

Here's a ritual to stop self-criticism in its tracks. If you repeat it regularly, you'll remember to stop blaming yourself for things that are out of your control and to stop feeling guilty when you've done your best.

You could use:

◆ Your phone, or a pen and paper

◆ An indulgent-as-you-like treat

Chances are you've heard the adage that when you're facing life's challenges you should speak to yourself in the same way you would to a friend, but it can be difficult to practise self-compassion. Carry out this ritual whenever you need to keep your inner critic under control.

Take a moment to reflect on how you're feeling and then send yourself a comforting text – and, yes, fill it with compassion as if you were writing to a friend. It may sound strange, but composing and typing a message like this can help you to reflect on things and to unlock your self-compassion.

Write whatever comes to mind and keep on going. If you want to target a specific situation, do that: "It's okay that you didn't get up early to go to the gym this morning – you deserve a lie-in now and then." Or if you need a general boost, remind yourself of your positive qualities: "You're a kind and thoughtful person. You always look out for others," and so on. (If you prefer, you can write your message down on paper.)

Read your words back when you've finished and let them sink in. Finish your ritual with a treat, be it your favourite hot drink, some chocolate, an episode of your latest boxset... or maybe all three!

A ritual for getting perspective

Intention: To make like an eagle and soar above your problems.

When you're in the midst of a difficult experience it can be hard to get perspective. This ritual will help you to see the bigger picture and can also stop you from dwelling on negative moments.

It's nice to perform this ritual outside if you can; somewhere with a view, where you can feel the wind on your face, is perfect. Sit comfortably and take a moment to settle in to your surroundings, feeling the ground beneath you and listening to the sounds of the natural world. Remember that you, too, are a part of this environment and a wonder of nature.

Focus on any birds that you can see and consider how it must feel to be a bird with the gift of flight. In pagan practice, birds of prey represent clear-sightedness: imagine yourself as a hawk or an eagle and soar up from the ground into the sky. Engage all your senses – how does it feel to have the sun warm your back or to ride on the wind?

Now look down on the earth below and see your surroundings from this perspective. What does the landscape look like? Can you see your home or place of work? (How tiny they must be.) Notice how, up here, you can only hear the sound of other birds or the wind. Look into the distance at the natural features of the landscape: the hillsides, rivers or fields. Visit them if you wish. Before you return to earth, remind yourself of your connection with this beautiful place and the things you love about it.

When you're ready, fly back down to your current resting place and take a few moments to readjust to a body without wings… but remember, you can always return to the skies whenever you need to.

A boring ritual

Intention: To embrace the
benefits of being bored.

With the whole world at our fingertips, it's easy to avoid boredom... but that's not necessarily a good thing. Over-stimulation means that our minds rarely have the downtime necessary to make sense of everything we've experienced, let alone give our thoughts a chance to surface.

This is the simplest ritual of all: you are going to practise doing nothing. Put down this book, sit on your hands and don't check your phone or flick on the TV. You don't need to focus on your breathing... you don't need to do anything at all. It might feel uncomfortable at first, but with practise you'll start to build up your resilience.

Human beings need to experience under-stimulation for the creative part of our brain to kick in, so give this ritual a try and see what your brain comes up with when you give it a chance to create its own entertainment.

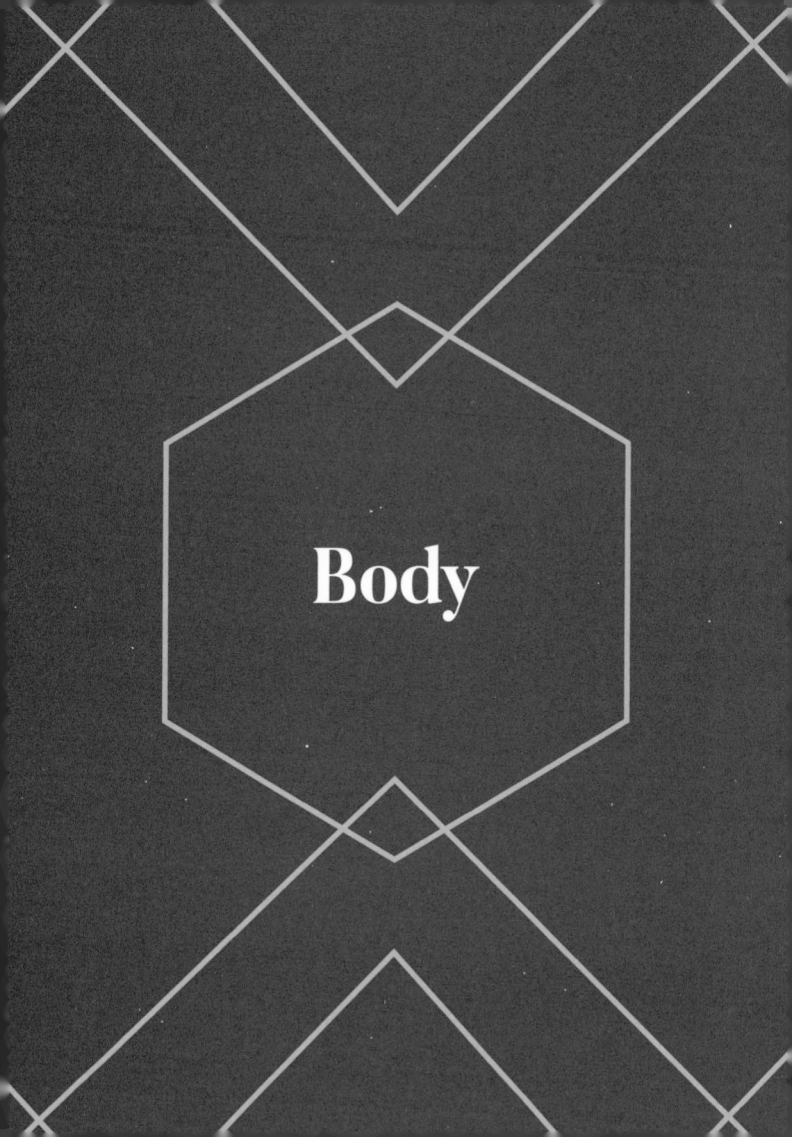

Body

A body-scan ritual

Intention: To focus on the present
moment and tune in to your body.

All you really need for this relaxing and restorative ritual is your
body, but you can enhance the experience and improve your
focus by burning some frankincense or cedarwood essential oil
(or by putting a few diluted drops on your third eye, the area just
above and between your brows).

Lie down – or sit, if it's more comfortable – and relax, releasing
any tension and letting your body sink into the floor or chair.
Focus on your breathing and the way your body changes as
you inhale and exhale. Notice the areas where your body is
touching the ground and bring your awareness to each of these
points in turn.

As you notice sensations in other areas of your body, focus on these: an ache, an area of tension, tingling, a difference in temperature. Let your body guide your mind and notice each in turn, experiencing it without judgement. You can "scan" your whole body if you wish, focusing on each part from the head down to the toes.

Before you finish, return your attention to your breathing. Imagine the oxygen you inhale flowing through your body as a whole, uniting all the parts you've been focusing on. When you're ready, tune back in to your surroundings and gently move your body before getting up.

This ritual will help you to release stress and to notice any areas of tension you might be holding. It will also teach you to refocus your mind during meditation. The more often you practise this, the easier it will become.

A foot-pampering ritual

Intention: To lavish your feet with
some well-deserved attention.

We cram them into unforgiving shoes, challenge them to walk 10,000 steps a day and hardly ever give them any appreciation... By taking time out to treat your feet, you'll be sure to slow down and relax – no checking emails or doing the ironing during your foot spa! You'll be giving your unconscious mind an important message, too: self-care is important and you deserve to be nurtured.

You could use:

- A large bowl
- 1–2 tbsp Epsom salts (or ¼ cup of milk)
- A foot scrub (or make your own with 2–3 tbsp rock salt, a glug of olive oil and a few drops of peppermint essential oil)
- A little olive oil
- Foot (or hand) cream
- Nail scissors/clippers and cuticle sticks
- Nail polish, if wanted

Get together everything you need – including some herbal tea to sip and a book to read while you relax – and light a candle or diffuse some drops of your favourite essential oil (lavender is relaxing). Have some music or a guided meditation cued up if you like, too.

Remove any traces of old nail polish from your toes and then soak your feet in a bowl of warm water with the Epsom salts or milk mixed in. Soak for at least ten minutes and relax completely.

Tackle any dead skin with your foot scrub and then rinse. Apply a little oil to your cuticles and push them back gently with the cuticle stick.

Trim your toenails (straight across) and massage moisturizer into your feet using a deep circular motion on the soles and slow but firm sweeping movements on the top of each foot. Massage the point above your heel to relieve stress. Finish by applying fresh nail polish, if you like.

A meaningful mealtime ritual

Intention: To slow down and savour each meal.

A mealtime ritual is a perfect way of introducing mindfulness to your day: eating is something that we do regularly and it involves using our senses, so pausing and focusing on the process every time is a good exercise. Even if you don't have time for a full sit-down meal, you can still benefit from eating your food in this way.

If you're preparing the food yourself, turn off any distractions and focus on the ingredients and your actions as you put your dish together. (Making repetitive tasks thoughtful is another excellent mindfulness exercise.)

Then have a definite transition between working and eating. Clear away any clutter from your eating area, close the door to the kitchen and lay out everything you need.

Before you eat, take a moment to pause and be thankful for the meal ahead. If you're eating with others, you might like to say aloud that you're grateful for the food on your plate. Even a little nod before you start eating, to mark the start of your meal, is a nice gesture.

Savour the flavours of your food by eating slowly and resting your cutlery between bites. Try to notice how you're feeling as you eat, too: learn to gauge when you're full and how different types of food make you feel. And finally, pause for a moment after your meal to appreciate it... before you head off to do the inevitable clearing up!

A tea-time
time-travel ritual

Intention: To revive and restore yourself
with an extra-special tea break.

How often do you make time for a proper tea break,
where you sit down and savour a drink? Taking a little time
out from the day – even if it's just five minutes – is a great
way to lower your stress levels. This ritual helps you to
make your tea break an oasis of calm in the middle of an
otherwise hectic day; a time to relax and take stock before
you tackle the next item on your to-do list. And by adding
some vintage touches you can enjoy the charm and calm
of a bygone era, too.

You could use:

- A pretty cup and saucer
- A teapot, strainer and milk jug
- Your favourite tea (or coffee)
- A historical novel

Take time to make your tea. While it's brewing, lay out your cup and saucer and add a couple of biscuits on the side for a fully authentic and indulgent experience. Find somewhere quiet and comfortable to relax with your tea – away from your work area if possible. To complete your time-travel experience, read a few pages of a novel set in your favourite era.

An exercise ritual

Intention: To tune in to your body and exercise mindfully.

Change your exercise time from a routine to a ritual and it will be more beneficial and enjoyable: you'll find yourself thinking of it as something positive that you've chosen to set aside time for, rather than something that has to be endured!

Before you start your session, listen to a favourite song to get you in the right frame of mind and mark the beginning of your workout – a calming track for yoga, or something upbeat that gets you ready for action if you're doing some cardio. You can do this while you put on your exercise gear, or while you get your water or any equipment ready. When combined, these are all great cues to prepare body and mind for your workout.

Have something in mind to focus on during your warm-up, something that reminds you of why you're exercising. It could be an inspirational picture that represents the results you want to achieve, or you might have a person or cause in mind that you're dedicating your efforts to.

Exercise mindfully: pay attention to how your body feels – the positive as well as the negative! Notice when your muscles are feeling stronger as you're repeating a move, or how your movements flow if you're completing sequences. And remember that, although exercise apps can be a great motivational tool, we're all different and feel different from day to day. So practise intuitive exercise and adapt what you're doing if you don't feel things are going to plan during a workout.

Celebrate the end of your workout by reflecting on all you've achieved as you cool down, enjoy some relaxing stretches and finish your ritual with a nutritious post-workout snack.

A ritual for better breathing

Intention: To check in with your breathing
and improve your technique.

This simple ritual will transform your day and improve your physical and mental well-being. Few of us breathe as deeply as we should, but by regularly focusing on our breathing we can learn to slow down, connect and take on board the right amount of oxygen.

Check in on your breathing throughout the day: on waking, before every meal and before bed, for example. (Use whatever cue suits you or set a reminder on your phone.) Each time, pause and think about where your breath is coming from: for many of us it will be high up in the chest, but we should be breathing from deeper down, toward the stomach. Aim to fill your lungs with smooth, slow breaths. Breathe in through the nose for five counts, hold for five and then release for five. Do this for a few minutes and, with regular practice, you'll improve your breathing technique.

A body-brushing ritual

Intention: To get your blood pumping
with some dry body brushing.

It takes very little time to make body brushing a part of your morning routine and enjoy all the benefits of improved circulation. Your skin will be smoother and look healthier; your immune system will receive a boost and you'll have more energy, too.

You could use:

◆ **A body brush with natural bristles**

◆ **Your usual moisturizer**

Spend a few minutes brushing before your shower in the morning. Use long smooth strokes starting with the soles of your feet, working up the legs and always brushing toward your heart. Brush from the hands up the arms and then finish with the chest, back and stomach, which can be brushed in a clockwise motion. Use a level of pressure that feels comfortable to you – brushing should leave your skin with a rosy glow – but take care with delicate areas. After brushing, shower as usual and then moisturize. Aim to brush around three times a week to notice the benefits.

A boost-your-diet ritual

Intention: To treat your body with
a superfood-filled day.

We all know that we should eat plenty of nutritious whole foods and cut back on processed meals and treats, but it's not always easy to do. Make a point of setting aside a day every week – or as often as you can – to give yourself a superfood nutritional boost. Plan ahead, remind yourself it's just for the day and then congratulate yourself on giving your body everything it needs (and not burdening it with anything it doesn't).

This boost day invites you to cut out processed sugars, saturated fats and red meat for 24 hours. Below is a suggested meal plan, but you can draw up your own. (For a vegan option swap out the dairy for your favourite plant-based substitutes.) To make your boost day more indulgent, why not make one of the meals a meal out? You could treat yourself to a superfood salad bowl at your local deli or health-food cafe.

Drinks: Green tea; water; hot water infused with lemon and ginger.

Breakfast: Porridge made with almond milk, sprinkled with mixed seeds and at least two handfuls of berries.

Lunch: A super salad of spinach and watercress, tomatoes, avocado, chopped carrots, peppers, olives and pomegranate seeds with either boiled eggs, tuna or scrambled tofu. Top with sunflower seeds and serve with rice cakes or cooked quinoa. Follow with two squares of dark chocolate.

Dinner: Fish or sweet potato stew made with lots of vegetables, passata, garlic, a variety of canned pulses, a handful of leafy greens and 1 tsp of turmeric. Served with brown rice and steamed vegetables (asparagus, broccoli or sugar snaps). Followed by plain Greek yogurt with 1 tsp of honey, topped with chopped nuts and fruit (such as plums, berries or dried apricots).

Snacks: Choose any of the following snacks: apple, pear, plum, a handful of almonds or mixed nuts, dried seaweed, a kefir drink.

A sleep-boosting ritual

Intention: To relax and enjoy
a peaceful night's sleep.

Repeating a relaxing sleep ritual every night before bed will boost your quality of sleep and make it much easier for you to drift off. (If you have problems sleeping, a regular routine is one of the best things you can introduce as it provides familiar cues to help you relax.) First make sure you have a good, calming end-of-the-day ritual in place (see p.96), with no screens, work, heavy meals or stressful tasks allowed in the hour or so before bed.

Make yourself a herbal tea containing valerian root – a natural sedative – or a cup of warm milk spiced with a pinch of nutmeg, which has a similar effect. Prepare your room by adjusting the lighting and the amount of bedding for maximum comfort. Either diffuse an essential oil blend that specifically promotes relaxation (such as vanilla or cedarwood); spray your pillow with a mist made from cooled boiled water and a few drops of lavender essential oil; or put a sleep spell bag under your pillow. (It could contain dried lavender tips; some lavender essential oil and an amethyst crystal, for example – all of these aid sleep.)

Carry out some basic yoga stretches: lie on your back with your legs leaning up against the wall and your arms relaxed at your sides, followed by Corpse Pose to give your body a gentle stretch and calm the mind. Finally, meditate if you wish: you could try a guided sleep meditation to help you drift off.

A health-burst ritual

Intention: To focus on your health
and nurture body, mind and
spirit in a purposeful way.

The ancient Chinese practice of Yang Sheng teaches people the importance of actively taking care of their health to prevent ailments from happening, rather than waiting for problems to develop and tackling them later on. It can be hard to prioritize our health, but this Yang Sheng-based ritual is easy to fit in to your day and can see off all sorts of stress-related ailments.

Go outside and take a brisk walk to get your blood flowing. Head for somewhere you can sit quietly for a moment or two.

Sit and connect with your environment: listen to the sounds around you and feel the sun on your skin.

Focus on your breathing, taking deep breaths and filling your lungs properly. This will boost your oxygen levels and leave you feeling more energized.

Gently massage the web of skin between your thumb and first finger on each hand. This acupressure point helps you to release any tension you're holding in your body.

Sip some water and eat some fruit. (A handful of berries, a peach or a plum are all low-GI snacks that are bursting with goodness and will give you a health boost.)

Finish your ritual with a smile to lift your mood and ease yourself back into your day.

A pampering bath ritual

Intention: To cleanse body and soul
with a luxurious salt bath.

Baths are so relaxing, and a luxurious bathing ritual is a great way to unwind at the end of the week. Salt baths are wonderfully restorative, too: they gently draw toxins out of the body and soak away any negativity that you've taken on during the week.

You could use:

- ◆ Tea lights or a scented candle
- ◆ Sea salt or rock salt (not table salt)
- ◆ Lavender essential oil
- ◆ Rose petals
- ◆ Your favourite face mask
- ◆ Herbal tea
- ◆ Soft music
- ◆ Even softer towels

Take a little time to get the bathroom ready for your ritual to make it as relaxing as possible. Gather everything you'll need, put on some soothing music and light your candles.

Before you take a soak, have a shower to cleanse fully and then run your bath, adding a couple of handfuls of good quality sea salt or Himalayan rock salt to the water (which should be warm but not too hot). You can also pop in a few drops of your favourite essential oil – lavender is a good choice to help you relax. Scatter some rose petals across the water for a truly luxurious experience.

Wash and exfoliate your face, and apply your face mask (a clay-based mask is great for detoxing). Then, step into the bath and soak away your troubles, letting go of any tensions and negativity. Don't forget to stay hydrated by sipping some water or herbal tea while you're bathing. When you've finished you might like to have another quick shower to rinse off any salt before wrapping yourself in soft towels and emerging from the bathroom feeling rejuvenated and ready for another week.

A yoga ritual

Intention: To practise a little yoga
every day, to stretch your body
and relax your mind.

A daily yoga ritual will benefit your mind, body and spirit. Yoga is very calming and it's also a naturally mindful activity. You focus on your breathing and your body as you enjoy the stretches and, of course, you improve your flexibility, too.

You might like to carry out your yoga ritual in the morning, perhaps as part of your greeting-the-day ritual (see p.72), as it puts you in a nice calm frame of mind before you get stuck in to your day's activities. Alternatively, you might prefer a few stretches to wind down before bed.

There are hundreds of yoga tutorials for beginners which can be found online, and even if you don't feel that you're very supple, there are some easy poses you can start with. Regular practice leads to great results, and you will soon notice your progress if you're repeating the same ritual.

A Sun Salutation is a lovely series of moves that flow into one another and stretch out the whole body, but if this is too complicated to start with you could simply try going from Mountain Pose to Chair Pose back to Mountain Pose and into Tree Pose, for example. For a floor-based yoga ritual try Downward Facing Dog, followed by Plank, a Cobra pose and Child's Pose to finish.

A better breakfast ritual

Intention: To enjoy the benefits of a
leisurely breakfast during the week.

Eating a proper breakfast means that you're less likely to over-indulge in the wrong foods later in the day. You'll also experience more stable energy levels and a better mood. And, if you make your breakfast a ritual, you'll enjoy the added bonus of a moment of calm, during which you can pause and focus on your own well-being before you tackle the day ahead.

If you would love to have a leisurely breakfast every day – instead of just at weekends – get up a little earlier and do it. Even fifteen minutes can make a difference to your whole day, so why not try it for a week and see if it suits you. Remember, you can do a little prep the night before by laying the table or mixing up a batch of overnight oats. A breakfast with few distractions is best: use the time to gather your thoughts and savour your food.

A de-stressing ritual

Intention: To release stress and instantly feel relaxed and calm.

If stress builds up it can cause all sorts of problems, so use this ritual whenever you feel tension rising to release it as it happens. You could even pick a trigger to remind you to carry it out – do it every time you boil the kettle, for example.

Start with a long steady out-breath to reset your breathing rate and instantly calm you. Then breathe slowly and steadily, in through the nose and out through the mouth for a few minutes.

Relax your jaw muscles, then unclench your shoulders. Roll your neck a few times, then relax your arms and hands. Unclench your back and core muscles, and finally relax your legs and feet.

Focus on this feeling of physical relaxation and continue to breathe slowly. Then finish your de-stressing ritual with one strong sigh to release any residual tension, followed by a big smile – an instant mood-booster!

An invigorating
head massage ritual

Intention: To de-stress and enjoy the benefits
of an ancient Indian treatment at home.

Based on the techniques of Indian head massage, this ritual will provide instant relaxation, alleviate headaches and boost the circulation. There's no need to use oil if you don't want to – all you really need are your hands – but you can use a little light olive oil, almond oil or coconut oil to add shine to your hair.

Put on some soothing music, find a suitable chair and burn your favourite incense. Put a towel around your shoulders and – if you're using it – warm your massage oil gently, adding a few drops of essential oil if you like.

Sit comfortably and then apply the oil (if using) to your hair. To distribute it evenly, divide your hair into sections: add some to the crown and spread it through your hair; then do the same starting at the nape of the neck. Once applied you're ready to begin the massage.

Start by gently rubbing your scalp all over, making small circular motions with your fingertips. Work from front to back, then back to front, and then massage each side. Repeat this whole process again. Next take small handfuls of your hair and gently tug these in turn to stimulate the scalp.

Now massage the temples, with as much pressure as feels comfortable, then move down to the top of the back. Massage your shoulders, too.

Finish by gently massaging the ears and applying a little pressure to the third eye acupressure point (above and between your brows) for a minute or so. You may like to wash your hair after this ritual if you've used oil.

A healthy-snacking ritual

Intention: To enjoy preparing nourishing and tasty snacks for the week ahead.

The key to healthy eating is to plan ahead, so it's a nice idea to make a ritual out of preparing some healthy snacks every weekend. Shut yourself away in the kitchen, put on some music and make yourself some tasty treats to relish throughout the week.

If you're a keen cook you might enjoy baking (think fibre-full flapjacks or a low-sugar banana bread), but if you're into low-prep snacking, making up your own portions of trail mix is easy and a money-saver, too.

Energy balls are a quick and easy snack to make ahead and great for getting you through the afternoon energy dip. There are lots of different variations on these, but this recipe is a good one to start with. It makes around 30 balls.

Chocolate, date and coconut energy balls

- ◆ **500 g (17 ½ oz) soft pitted dates**
- ◆ **100 g (3 ½ oz) cocoa powder**
- ◆ **75 g (2 ½ oz) desiccated coconut**

Soften the dates in a bowl of just-boiled water. Drain and rinse with cold water then add to your blender with the cocoa powder and desiccated coconut. Pulse until smooth, adding in a tablespoon of hot water partway through to bring the mixture together if necessary.

Shape into balls and then roll in a little more desiccated coconut to coat. Chill the balls, then store them in the fridge in a sealed container for up to a week, or freeze them. (They can be defrosted in the fridge overnight.)

Once you've given these a try, you could experiment with different ingredients, including nuts, seeds, oats and chopped dried fruit. Why not try a different recipe every time?

A time-out-from-time ritual

Intention: To tune in to your body's biorhythms and plan your activities around them.

It's likely that the routine you follow for your day is not a natural fit with your body rhythms. Most of us have to get up at a particular time for work, or must eat and sleep to fit around our commitments, and few of us can take a nap when our body needs an energy boost most – in the middle of the afternoon.

This ritual invites you to spend a day or two letting your body guide you as to when you should eat, sleep and exercise. It may not be practical to follow it often, but if you complete it occasionally at the weekend or when you have a few days off, you'll become more familiar with your body's rhythms and can attune your activities more closely to them during the week.

Pick a day when you don't have any commitments, avoid any distractions, and perhaps even turn off your phone. Make the day as mindful as possible and try to avoid any alcohol or caffeine, which could affect your natural cycles. Get up when you feel rested; eat when you feel hungry (let your body decide what) and nap if you need to. When you're most alert, carry out any work that's needed; when you're full of energy head out for a brisk walk or run. Don't forget to factor in time for meditation and relaxation.

It can take time to find your natural rhythm. Carry out this ritual for a few days in a row if possible, then see if you can apply some of what you've learned to your normal weekly routine. Perhaps you'll discover that getting up early and doing the housework first thing works best for you; or maybe you'll feel more energized if you eat your main meal at lunchtime rather than in the evening.

A ritual for when you're ill

Intention: To take time out to recuperate and nurture yourself when you need to.

One of the worst things you can do when you're coming down with a cold or bug is to soldier on, ignoring your symptoms. By planning a self-care ritual for those days when you're feeling unwell, you can make sure you recover as quickly as possible.

You could use:

◆ Herbal tea

◆ Nutritious snacks

◆ Some boiling water and tea-tree oil

◆ A good book

◆ A little patience

As soon as you start to feel unwell, make an effort to stay hydrated, drinking plenty of water or herbal tea. Keep your Vitamin C and zinc levels up and try to opt for nourishing foods, such as veggie-packed broths. Berries, kiwi fruit, bananas, spinach and fish are all superfoods that can boost your immune system and help you to fight off a cold, so try to include some of these if you feel up to it.

If you're feeling too ill to work, you shouldn't do it! Remind yourself that it's important to prioritize getting better, otherwise you could end up taking more time off in the long run. Call in sick, rearrange any plans and rest.

If you're congested, inhaling the steam from a basin of hot water with a few added drops of tea-tree oil should help. (Alternatively, use a nasal saline spray or simply have a hot shower.) Take your meds when necessary and have a hot-water bottle to hand for any aches and pains.

Try to see your time out of action as a time to tune in to your body, nurture yourself and prioritize your well-being. Try some simple de-stressing rituals, too, such as a Grounding Ritual (p.76) or a Ritual for Better Breathing (p.46), as worrying about what you should be doing could slow up your recovery. Get well soon!

A make-a-shake ritual

Intention: To prepare and relish
a nutritious shake or smoothie.

A smoothie a day is a great way to boost your intake of vitamins and minerals. When you add in superfood ingredients, such as turmeric or saffron, you're treating your body to powerful natural anti-inflammatories, too. Make your smoothie ritual extra special by taking time to choose your ingredients and prepare your drink; having a special glass – or chalice – to drink it in; and by savouring your shake once it's ready.

Some nutritious smoothie
ingredients include:

- Avocado
- Banana
- Berries
- Chia seeds

- Dates
- Ginger
- Goji berries
- Hemp seeds
- Kelp
- Mango
- Oats
- Raw honey
- Saffron (a pinch)
- Spinach
- Turmeric

Experiment with flavours or look online for smoothie inspiration. There are plenty of delicious options that will leave you feeling energized and give you a nutrient boost. You could try banana with a couple of dates, a teaspoon each of turmeric and cinnamon and a cup of milk, for example. Don't forget that you can go vegan by using almond or coconut milk (or any other plant-based alternative), or by simply whizzing up some favourite fruits with a little apple juice, orange juice or coconut water. Remember to keep a record of your favourite combinations.

A ritual to boost your energy

Intention: To beat the afternoon dip and re-energize.

Our bodies go through a daily cycle of energy, with dips in the early hours of the morning and in the middle of the afternoon. Chances are that it's the mid-afternoon slump that you'll notice most, so develop a pick-me-up ritual to boost your energy at this time (unless you can have a catnap to recharge your batteries – but no more than 15–20 minutes, or you'll feel more drained than when you dropped off!).

Your afternoon energy-boost ritual could include a change of scenery, especially if you've been staring at a screen (try five minutes outside practising breathwork – see p.46), having a stretch, a glass of water, a cup of herbal tea or a fruit snack. You could include a burst of energetic activity: a brisk walk around the block or a dance to some music. You may want to avoid eating a heavy lunch, too, as this will make you feel sleepier.

Spirit

A greeting-the-day ritual

Intention: To create a peaceful and
positive start to your day.

Mornings can be such a chaotic time, and they tend to set the
pace for the day ahead. This ritual will help you to practise a little
self-care in the morning and ensure that you leave home in a
calm and positive frame of mind.

Start by setting your alarm a little earlier than usual, so that you
feel rested rather than rushed when you begin your day, and
wake to natural daylight if you can. Make the most of those first
moments after waking when you're naturally relaxed: let your
mind wander and follow its train of thought, noting where it
flows. Then give it a little direction toward something positive –
focus on the fact that you are safe, happy or warm.

When you get up, try to make sure your first encounter is with nature. Spend a few moments looking out of the window or, even better, go outside and sit quietly for five minutes, connecting with nature before you connect with the Wi-Fi!

Include some stretches in your morning ritual if possible. You could simply straighten your spine, raise your arms and reach for the sky; or why not try a few Sun Salutations (see p.56). Finish by giving your arms a rub and hugging yourself.

Before you get on with your usual morning routine, it's nice to pick a positive intention to guide your day (or draw a guidance card, see p.78). You could choose "I can't wait to see what today brings," or "I can take every challenge in my stride,"... whatever seems pertinent to you. If you prefer, you could simply pick a mood for the day ahead – happiness or excitement or peace – and tune in to this whenever you can. This will help you to take control of your day and choose how you want to experience it, rather than getting caught up in other people's chaos.

A ritual to help you move on

Intention: To take control and move on from
a relationship or emotive situation.

It can be hard to move on from situations that have been
important to us, especially if we've invested a lot of energy in
them. If you feel that it's time to move on but can't quite make
the break, doing something symbolic can help you to take
control and find closure. A long-standing connection may not
be severed overnight; this ritual is carried out over consecutive
evenings until you feel you've made progress.

You could use:

 ◆   A white candle

 ◆   A piece of paper and pen

 ◆   A red ribbon

 ◆   A pair of scissors

 ◆   A heatproof dish

 ◆   Some sprigs of rosemary

Light the candle and then write the name of the person or situation you wish to leave behind on the piece of card. Tie the ribbon around your wrist. Focusing on the card, spend a few moments reflecting on your situation, then think of the elements you wish to release. You may say these aloud if you like: "Unhappiness, I let you go," for example. Finish by saying the name of the person or situation followed by "I let you go." Extinguish the candle, untie the ribbon and put them away with the piece of card until the following evening.

Repeat this ritual over at least four nights. (For extra potency, you could carry out this ritual during the fortnight when the moon is waning – as the moon fades, so will your unwanted connection.)

When you feel ready, carry out the ritual one final time, but finish by taking the card and setting it alight in the candle flame as you name and release your situation. Let the card burn in the heatproof dish along with the rosemary sprigs. Now snip the ribbon from your wrist, saying "I am free." Take the ashes from the dish outside with the piece of ribbon and bury them.

A grounding ritual

Intention: To reconnect with nature and recharge your spiritual batteries.

This ritual is wonderfully effective and calming – and it's so simple to do. It's the perfect antidote to the busy rush of modern living: by taking a few moments out to reconnect with mother nature you'll feel calmer and happier and you'll be in a much better position to carry on with your day. (If you can't get outside, you can still use the same visualization indoors to good effect.)

Go outside to a comfortable spot where you can stand on the grass – barefoot is best, if possible. Close your eyes, feel your connection with the earth and take a moment to focus on your breathing. Take slow and steady breaths: feel invigorating energy flowing into your lungs and around your body as you inhale. When you exhale, breathe out slowly, picturing any sluggish energy or negativity leaving your body.

Focus on your contact with the ground and imagine your feet sinking a little into the earth. Now picture roots extending from your feet deep into the soil. Picture them threading down farther and farther into the ground, anchoring you safely like a tree. Every time you breathe in feel warm, nurturing energy flowing up into your body through these roots. As you exhale, picture this energy flowing out through the crown of your head and your fingertips, as if they were branches.

Once you're feeling balanced and calm, imagine your roots gently retracting back into your body. Move your feet slowly, and refocus on the sounds and sights around you. As you practise this ritual more often you'll find it easy to tap in to this lovely source of calming energy whenever you need it.

A guidance card ritual

Intention: To tune in to your inner thoughts through tarot or oracle cards.

This ritual, in which you draw a guidance card for the day, is a perfect way to tap in to your thoughts and inner wisdom. There's nothing "spooky" about oracle cards: they simply contain images for you to reflect on. How you feel about each image will depend on your own experiences and concerns at the time. This makes them wonderful tools for giving your subconscious a voice.

If you don't already own a pack of oracle cards, choose a set that appeals to you. Do a little online research to find a theme that interests you, then check out the illustrative style. Sit quietly and hold your deck in your hands. Take a moment to ground yourself and clear your mind of any distractions: close your eyes, breathe deeply and focus on your breath.

Shuffle the cards and draw one from the pack – if a card leaps out at you while you're shuffling, the deck has chosen for you! Look at the image and note your instant reaction to it before you examine it in detail. Does the card make you feel excited, perplexed, reassured? If there's a figure in the illustration, who do they remind you of?

Think about how the card could be pertinent to you before you reach for the guidebook that comes with the pack. Your personal reaction is always very revealing. Read up on the symbolism of the image and think about it as you go through your day. You may like to display the card (on your altar, if you have one) or take a picture of it and keep it on your phone.

The more often you work with your cards, the stronger their associations will become, so repeating this ritual – and making a note about your card and its relevance in your journal – is very rewarding.

A ritual for
setting intentions

Intention: To focus on creating
and pursuing clear intentions.

This ritual will help you to commit to new projects and to
stay motivated as you work toward your goals. The new
moon is a great time to set intentions, particularly those
relating to new projects and fresh starts.

You could use:

- Lemon balm incense

- A red or orange candle

- Your journal, or a cork board and pins,
  plus any pictures that represent your
  intentions

- Pen and paper

- A selection of crystals (for example
  quartz, citrine, amazonite)

- A small bowl

Clear an area to use for your ritual and dedicate it to your intentions for the month ahead. (Smudge with sage if you like, to dispel any stale energy – see p.84.) Burn some lemon balm incense to promote clarity, and meditate on the intention(s) you wish to set. Write them down in your journal and be really specific. If you want a new job, what is it you're looking for exactly? Do you have a particular role in mind? Letting your pen run away with you is an important part of this ritual as it helps you to tune in to your enthusiasm. (If you prefer, create a mood board instead and fill it with pictures that symbolize what you want to achieve.)

Light a red or orange candle to remind you of the energy needed to fuel your passions. Now write out your intentions again on slips of paper and fold these. Put them in a small bowl and surround this with crystals (such as quartz for amplifying your energy, citrine for manifestation or amazonite for courage and enthusiasm). Add oracle cards drawn while meditating on your wishes, if you like.

Whenever you have time, light the candle and check in with your intentions. Look through your journal and remind yourself of why you want to achieve your goal. Record your progress as you go – and don't forget to celebrate each achievement along the way, too.

A ritual for connecting with your animal guide

Intention: To invite animal energy into your life and use it to enhance your spirituality.

Pagan traditions teach us that we have animal guides at our side offering us energy and support. This is a comforting thought and meditating on which animal(s) you have a connection with can be a calming and revealing experience.

Most of us have a connection with animals in some way, so if you already feel drawn to a species, research its symbolism and reflect on how these traits relate to you. You might like to find an object that represents your animal and add this to your meditation space to remind you of these qualities.

Many people believe we're drawn to different animals at different stages in our lives. A meditation can help you to connect with your animal guide and is simple to try.

Find a comfortable place to meditate and settle down to focus on your breathing. As you do so, state your intention: to meet your animal companion. Picture yourself in the centre of a stone circle and imagine your surroundings. Perhaps you can feel the warmth of a great stone at your back. When you're ready, invite your animal guide to come forward into the circle, and see what happens next. Allow your subconscious to take the lead: you may feel able to interact with your guide and ask if they have a message for you. Maybe you'll watch them, or simply sit with them and sense their energy. When you feel ready, thank them for their presence and re-focus on the physical world around you. Note down your experiences afterward.

If you don't sense an animal at all, don't despair. It can take a few attempts to relax into the meditation. Or you might find that your animal turns up later in a dream, a news story or another area of your life, so look out for them!

A ritual for
brushing off negativity

Intention: To banish negativity
with a spiritual detox.

Carry out this ritual whenever you've had a difficult day to brush off any negativity you've brought home with you.

You could use:

◆ A sage smudging stick or

◆ Sage essential oil diluted in cooled boiled water

As soon as you get home, take off your coat and put your bags away, then ground yourself by sitting quietly and feeling your body sinking into your chair. Focus on your breathing for a moment. Now light a sage smudging stick and pass this around your body to smudge away any negative vibes. (Sage has long been used to clear away negative energies.) Alternatively you can add ten drops of sage essential oil to a two-ounce glass spray bottle of water and spray this around yourself instead. Finish your ritual with a cleansing shower or a soak in a salt bath (see p.54).

A gratitude ritual

Intention: To relive the high
points of your day.

It's important to spend time reflecting on the positive experiences we've had during the day – without this sort of focus, our minds can be drawn to negative, self-critical thoughts. Studies have shown that looking on the bright side is something we can train our brains to do, and that people who take a "glass half-full" approach are much less likely to suffer from stress or depression.

An easy-to-follow ritual is to start a gratitude journal and write something in it every evening. Don't feel pressure to list three things every night; if just one high-point comes to mind, focus on that and record it in whatever way works best for you – with a few words, a cartoon or a page-long anecdote. Practise this regularly and you'll find yourself recognizing these positive moments as they happen... and maybe even going out and looking for them.

A ritual to help you accept your flaws

Intention: To abandon self-doubt and embrace every aspect of what makes you, you.

One of the most positive things you can do is to learn to accept your flaws, be they physical, temperamental or spiritual. When you do this you stop comparing yourself with others and questioning your self-worth. This beautiful, empowering ritual will help you to achieve this. It's nice to carry it out once a month – you could tie it in with the full moon, which is a fitting time to recognize how brilliant you are.

You could use:

◆ A mirror – the larger, the better

◆ A pink candle

◆ Oak leaves (or slips of paper) and a pen

◆ A small vase or pot

Find somewhere quiet and set up your mirror so that you can sit comfortably in front of it. Light the candle and still your mind by focusing on your breathing.

When you're ready to begin, stare at your reflection in the mirror. Start by looking directly into your eyes and holding your own gaze for a minute or so. Let your judgements drift away as you focus on the unique soul that you see looking back at you. Feel love and respect for yourself and all you have achieved. Now widen your gaze to take in the rest of your reflection and see yourself as a whole, sending fondness and gratitude to your physical form.

When you're ready to finish, take an oak leaf and write on it a characteristic you've recognized in yourself. (Oak leaves are a symbol of strength.) Write down as many as you can – try not to judge these as positive or negative, simply note each one down on a leaf. Store the leaves in your pot. (It's a nice touch to choose a pot that's a little flawed – it is, after all, these kinds of individual quirks that make things so special.) Repeat the ritual whenever you need to appreciate what makes you unique.

A good-luck ritual

Intention: To charge up an amulet
with good-luck vibes.

In many spiritual traditions, an amulet is seen as a powerful charm for bringing good luck to the wearer. It's easy to create your own amulet and make it a symbol of positivity. Your amulet will help you to practise positive thinking when you need a good-luck boost and give you the best chance of success.

First choose (or make) a necklace with a charm that symbolizes good luck to you. You could search for inspiration online, use a favourite crystal or choose a token that represents your animal companion (see p.82) – picking a talisman that is meaningful to you is the most important thing.

Next, charge your amulet with good luck: this can be done by simply meditating on it, if you wish. Relax and ground yourself, then visualize a bright stream of energy from the source of life itself flowing into your necklace, and focus on this feeling of positivity and power.

If you wish, you can also bless your talisman with the four elements of pagan tradition – earth, water, air and fire. Sprinkle a little sand on your amulet for earth; then anoint it with some water; pass it through some incense for air and finally across a candle flame for fire. Finish by visualizing the bright energy of spirit flowing into your amulet.

Wear your amulet whenever you need a good-luck boost. Pause before you head off into your challenging situation, touch your amulet and close your eyes for a moment, thinking back to your blessing meditation or ceremony. This will help you to tune in to its power. You can repeat the blessing ritual whenever you need to keep your amulet – and your own positivity – topped up.

A mantra ritual

Intention: To use the power of mantras to boost your well-being and change your negatives to positives.

By repeating mantras – positive phrases or specific sounds – we can change our mindset for the better. To aid meditation you can start with a simple sound, such as "om", and concentrate on repeating this. It will give your mind something to focus on, and move it away from negative thoughts or mental chatter. For targeting negativity or tackling a particular issue you can choose your own specific power mantra. Pick a simple phrase to suit your needs: "I am strong"; "I will do it"; "I feel peace or; "I have everything I need to succeed." You can also adapt your mantra as you work toward a goal, if appropriate. You could start with "I am building my confidence every day" and move on to "I am confident", for example.

Practise your mantra daily as part of your morning or evening ritual if you can. If you diffuse your favourite essential oil before you start, you'll build a powerful association between the scent and your words, which can be useful at other times. For example, you could wear a dab of this oil, suitably diluted, on your pressure points – your wrists or temples – and the scent will help you to tune in to your mantra energy throughout the day.

Relax and steady your breathing, focusing on the aroma you've chosen. Now repeat your mantra (in your head or aloud) and let your words link-up with the rhythm of your breathing – repeating them on every out-breath, for example. As you repeat your chosen words, focus on the sound of each one and the feeling of the phrase as a whole – whether it's courage, peace or patience. Repeat this exercise daily to release the power of your mantra.

A ritual for
sensing your aura

Intention: To sense and see your aura.

All living things have an energy field around them: something you might already pick up on when you sense another person's "vibes" or if you get intuitive feelings about them. Carrying out this ritual regularly will teach you to tune in to these feelings more easily and to discover your own aura. It's a really rewarding spiritual experience, which can help you to heal, to make decisions and to build relationships. It's a big topic, but start with this basic aura ritual and you'll have good skills to build on.

Begin by learning to sense the first layer of your aura. Sit quietly and ground yourself. Imagine a column of bright white energy extending down through the crown of your head, along your spine and into the ground. You are now connected to the primary source of energy that animates living things: feel this flowing down your arms and into your hands. Rub your hands together rapidly, then hold your palms about six inches apart and feel them buzzing with energy. Gradually move your hands closer together until you feel a gentle resistance between your palms: this is the innermost layer of your aura. (It may be quite close to your skin.)

Once you've learned to feel your aura, you can try viewing it by repeating the exercise, this time holding your hand in front of an off-white background after you've rubbed your palms together. Bring your thumb and forefinger together into a "C" shape and stare at the area between them. Now focus the loving energy that's flowing through your arm down into that spot. It may take a few attempts but persevere and you should see auric energy as a haze or blur around your hand. The more you practise, the easier it gets. You can try this anywhere, so give it a go regularly to boost your skills. You may want to develop these further and go on to investigate the many ways you can use aura-reading in your day-to-day life.

A ritual for attracting prosperity

Intention: To invite abundance actively into your life.

Most of us have, at some time or another, found ourselves wishing to be more prosperous, but if we don't do anything to pursue this actively, our circumstances are unlikely to change. Set up a space in your home to carry out this ritual and focus on your intention, and you're much more likely to experience the feelings of abundance that you wish for.

You could use:

- A green candle
- A money plant
- A small decorative saucer
- A single shiny coin
- An image of a deity, person or symbol that represents wealth to you
- Some small squares of red paper

Choose a place in the home to set up your prosperity altar. Whether on a window ledge or the corner of a coffee table, it's important to have a permanent, designated place to honour your blessings and invite prosperity.

Clean the area with a witch-hazel spray (see p.16) or a little rose water and then arrange your items on your altar. Inscribe the candle with any symbols that represent prosperity to you, and pop the coin into the saucer. Light the candle and take a moment to pause and think of the blessings in your life for which you're already grateful. Write some of these down on the little squares of paper and add them to the dish.

Every day, take a moment to honour your blessings and your wishes in this space. Light the candle, tend your plant and add blessing slips to the dish when you think of them. (You can add any crystals or other items that symbolize prosperity to the saucer too, if you like.) Refresh your altar when you need to, and relish the blessings that come your way.

An end-of-the-day ritual

Intention: To slow down, shed your worries and relax at the end of the day.

Whether you've spent a hectic day at work, rushed around at home tackling your to-do list or been inundated with media input for an hour or two, it can be hard to wind down and relax in the evening. Carry out this ritual to mark the transition from a busy day to some calm and reflective moments before bed. You could use the time afterward for journaling, reading, meditating or to just drift off into a contented sleep.

You could use:

- Lavender essential oil
- Paper, pencil and a jar
- Herbal tea

Take a relaxing bath, if you've time, and add a few drops of lavender essential oil to the water. While the water's running, tidy away any reminders of the day's tasks and turn off your phone, then let the water soak away your tension and stress.

After your bath, change into comfortable clothing and jot down a note of anything that's on your mind – specific worries or a list of tasks you need to complete the next day. Fold up your list, put it in the jar and store it out of sight.

Now make yourself a cup of herbal tea, light a candle and relax. Your downtime starts here – and even if it's just ten minutes, you'll benefit from it enormously. You might choose to do some yoga stretches (see p.56) and a guided meditation (there are plenty of apps which provide these) or to settle down with your journal or a good book. Whatever you do, pick something that you love and give it your full attention.

It's a nice idea to have a shortened version of this ritual in mind for those evenings when you don't have as much time as you would like. For example: a quick shower, a tidy away of the day's tasks, some stretches and a moment reflecting on the most positive part of your day.

A ritual for letting go of the little things

Intention: To release everyday irritations as they crop up.

Little gripes can add up throughout the week and it's all too easy to dwell on them. This ritual can be carried out regularly to rid you of any annoyances that have cropped up – and as it involves going outside, you'll experience the healing power of nature at the same time.

Take a trip to a nearby river, pond or the seaside and pick a stone for every angsty feeling or event you wish to release. One by one, take each stone in your hand and think about how the situation makes you feel. Now throw it out into the water as far as you can, releasing all the negative energy that has built up around it. Repeat until you're out of stones, then breathe in the fresh air and dive back into your day feeling rejuvenated.

Creative
Rituals

A ritual for inviting inspiration

Intention: To seek out inspiration from wise and wonderful sources.

Tapping in to the wisdom of others is a brilliant way to expand our own horizons. Other people's stories can help us to put our experiences into perspective, teach us how to handle tricky situations or even inspire us to go out and change our lives. Carrying out a regular inspiration ritual will benefit you enormously and is enjoyable, too. It doesn't need to be a long session – the important thing is that you actively seek out wisdom and then give your "guru" your full attention the whole time.

You could try:

TED talks – a great place to start. The website (www.ted.com) has plenty of short talks by inspiring people to pique your interest.

An inspirational book – read the autobiography of someone you admire, research motivational stories or turn to a book of inspirational quotes.

Find a mentor – perhaps there's someone you know already who always gives good advice or has a broad experience of life. Spend time with them when you can.

When you've finished your conversation or inspirational session, take a few moments to reflect on it before you get diverted. Can you sum up their story or wisdom in a sentence? Or even a single word? Write this down in your journal to keep a record of what you learn, and don't be afraid to tell others about it and pass your wisdom forward.

A blanket-making ritual

Intention: To craft a comforting meditation blanket.

Crafts such as knitting, crochet and sewing are very soothing and offer us benefits similar to those we might get from meditation. The activities give us something to focus our attention on, as well as a sense of achievement when we finish each part of our project.

The goal of this ritual is to make a blanket mindfully, which you might like to use during meditation. You may have a favourite craft already, so pick whichever appeals to you most: knitting, crocheting or making patchwork pieces to stitch together. If you don't yet have crafting experience, now is the time to learn!

You can easily access tutorials on YouTube, but crafting with others is great fun, so why not book in a few lessons with the talented knitter in your family or try a taster session at a local craft shop. (Please don't feel that this project is too complicated for a beginner: it's possible to crochet a large rug with just three basic stitches and no need for sewing pieces together, so don't be put off!)

You could work on your blanket during your quiet time before bed. Add to it little by little, putting your love, energy and attention into your work, and you will enjoy these blessings when you use the blanket during meditation. When it's finished, you might like to decorate it with charms and feathers and anoint the corners with a little of your favourite essential oil, so that you have the comforting scent to hand during meditation.

A three-smiles-a-day ritual

Intention: To create happiness and spread it with the power of a smile.

The act of smiling – even when we don't feel we have anything to smile about – will boost our mood; and smiling reduces our stress levels and blood pressure, too. While children may smile up to 400 times a day, by adulthood the happiest among us may only smile 40 times, and for the rest of us it's even less. So remind yourself to smile regularly with this little ritual and you'll feel the benefits – and share them with the people you meet, too!

Your daily goal is to:

- Make yourself smile
- Make a loved-one smile
- Make a stranger smile

Whether you watch a clip of your favourite comedy show or keep a "smile file" of articles and pictures that make you laugh, find yourself something to smile about every day... and if you can't do that, just look yourself in the eye in the mirror, give yourself a big, beaming smile and feel your spirits rise.

It's easy enough to make others smile, too, as a smile shared will soon spread, but you might like to find more creative ways of hitting your daily smile quota. If you're finding it too easy, up your smile count or go one better and create a laughter ritual – laughing has even more benefits than smiling.

A what-would-Jane-Eyre-do? ritual

Intention: To invite your hero to help you face your challenges.

This ritual is a creative way of getting some perspective on challenging situations and looking at them from another point of view. Although it's a fun exercise to do, there's some logic behind it, too. Often, the people we admire most possess the characteristics we would love to cultivate in ourselves, and tuning in to them can help us to take a strong and considered approach to our challenges.

You could use:

◆   Writing materials

◆   Your imagination

Start by writing down a brief summary of your situation. Next identify someone you admire – it could be Jane Eyre, James Bond or your best friend – a favourite fictional character or your real-life hero. Pause a moment to consider their character traits and why you admire them, then have fun writing the story of your situation or encounter with your hero taking your place. How would they handle things? What would the ultimate outcome be? Let your imagination loose and write your tale in whatever form takes your fancy.

Afterward, read it through and see if any aspects of your story are useful to you back in the real world. Even if you can't have Katniss Everdeen at your side fighting your battles, you can tap in to a little of her energy when you're facing your office nemesis!

A find-your-flow ritual

Intention: To discover and enjoy
your favourite flow activities.

Flow activities are the things you get so caught up in that you lose
track of time. They're challenging, rewarding and absorbing – and
this means that doing them regularly is beneficial for us mentally
and even physically, with studies showing that they defuse stress,
promote self-esteem and boost our mental skills, too.

Spend a little time thinking about which activities trigger a flow
state for you. For some people it's sports, for others it's creative
or artistic pursuits, or it may be reading or completing puzzles.
It could be something you enjoyed as a child – or maybe it's a
hobby you've yet to discover, so do some experimenting.

Whatever it is, you should enjoy the challenge of your activity, be confident that you can complete it and – most of all – become so absorbed in it that you'll feel as though a whole hour has flown past in the space of a few minutes. (Warning: not all flow activities are wholesome, so try to pick something that won't have a negative impact on your well-being!)

Now make time to engage in your chosen activity (or activities) as regularly as you can and make a ritual of each session. Turn off any distractions first; get everything you need to hand and focus solely on going with the flow, enjoying the sense of engagement and accomplishment that your session will bring.

A drumming ritual

Intention: To de-stress with some therapeutic drumming.

Drumming is an effective way to release stress, promote healing and rejuvenate your mind, body and soul. It works so well because it's an activity that uses both sides of the brain and synchronizes them. (We use the rational side of our brain to process rhythms and the creative side to appreciate them.) Drumming slow, repetitive patterns can also help us to experience an "alpha wave" state in the brain, the relaxed state we achieve during meditation.

You can benefit by simply listening to meditative drumming, but trying it yourself is great fun. Start with a simple, steady beat – use your thighs or a tabletop if you don't have a drum! Breathe in time to your drum strokes and really focus on the sound and the sensation of your hand striking the surface you're using. Whether you drum when you're feeling tense or as a way to wind down every night before bed, you'll notice the benefits of your session straightaway.

A ritual for nurturing a plant

Intention: To strengthen your connection
with the rhythm of the natural world.

Growing plants helps us to tune in to nature and to slow down. It's even been shown that spending time around plants can boost your immune system. Whether you've got a windowsill or a whole plot at your disposal, you can incorporate a gardening ritual into your lifestyle and enjoy the benefits, too.

If you're new to gardening, start small with some potted herbs and harvest these to make your own tea. If you have bigger plans, how about some tomatoes in a window box, or a raised bed of veggies outside. A flowering plant will brighten up your room and can still be nurtured (and spoken to, if you wish). Pick something with a wonderful perfume – such as a polyanthus – and you can enjoy the aroma, too.

Make a ritual of checking in with your plant every day. Care for it when needed, or meditate on it for a really calming experience.

A pause-for-poetry ritual

Intention: To find comfort, peace
and beauty in poetry.

Words are powerful, and good poetry will weave a spell of sound and emotion for you to tap into whenever you wish. Forget any childhood memories of being asked to search for meaning and metaphor in dusty old stanzas – although many classical poems are very beautiful – you don't need to analyze a poem to enjoy it. (Song lyrics are poetry, after all, and many of us find it easy to enjoy and appreciate those.)

This ritual asks you to explore and ponder poetry – all you need to do it is an enquiring mind, and perhaps your journal to record some favourite quotes. You could even start with your best-loved song lyrics: write them out in your journal and illustrate them, or think about what they mean to you.

If you're new to poetry, take a look at poemhunter.com or poetryfoundation.org for some initial inspiration and find a poem that interests you. You may like to memorize a verse or two, as repeating poetry can be very calming.

Reading a poem aloud is often the best way to experience it, as poems are designed to be performed, or you can watch performances on YouTube. Many bars and cafes have open mic nights, too, where you can experience poetry live. You might not love everything you hear, but the evening will still fire up your creative mind – you may even decide to write something of your own.

A soap-making ritual

Intention: To embark on a mindful and creative soap-making project.

Hand-making soap is the perfect project to nourish your mind, body and soul: you get to unleash your creativity; you can imbue your soaps with decorative touches and positive vibes and, of course, you will end up with a lovely product that doesn't include harsh additives.

Once you've invested in a few basics, you can have a ritual soap-making session once a month and customize the soaps you make for the month ahead: you could make lavender soap if you're facing a stressful couple of weeks; or a cleansing oatmeal and honey soap for the new year. These soaps make perfect gifts, too. There are dozens of ideas for different soap recipes online, and you'll soon come up with your own favourite combinations.

Making soap from scratch involves using lye, but this can be complicated for beginners, so an easy way to get up and running is to use a pre-made soap base. This recipe for lavender and oatmeal soap is a good first project and will make two medium-sized bars. (These will be delicately scented – if you prefer a stronger scent, use a little more essential oil.)

You could use:

◆ 400 g (14 oz) melt-and-pour soap base

◆ 60 g (2 oz) rolled oats

◆ 1 tbsp dried lavender buds

◆ 1/2 tsp lavender essential oil (about 100 drops)

◆ Shop-bought soap moulds (or use silicone muffin cases or yoghurt containers)

Cut your soap base into chunks and melt these in a jug in the microwave. (It's best to do this in 15-second bursts.) Once melted, let the soap cool for a minute, then stir in the rolled oats and lavender buds. Add the essential oil and pour into moulds. Leave the bars to cool for several hours, then you can finish the process in the fridge. Once chilled, pop the soap out of the moulds, wrap – in greaseproof paper, an organza bag or a soap box – and store ready to enjoy in the coming weeks.

A learning ritual

Intention: To learn a new skill
with focus and intention.

Many of us would love to learn a new skill and probably have a list of things we'd like to try but have never got around to doing. There's plenty of research that shows the benefits of learning something new – from increasing confidence and beating depression to boosting our brain power and concentration.

Making a ritual of learning can encourage you to find the time to pursue your goals and make sure that you get the most of your study session. Once you've decided what you'd like to learn, set aside a regular time slot for your ritual. (Remember, you don't have to find hours every week – you might be able to listen to podcasts on your commute, use your language app for 15 minutes at lunchtime or get up half an hour early once a week and hit the books before you get absorbed in your day.)

If you are able to set aside a dedicated area to study, make this as welcoming as possible by using good lighting and making sure you have somewhere comfortable to sit. The routine of setting up your space before you begin each session will become a good trigger to prepare your mind for "learning mode". You could make a cup of herbal tea and also diffuse some essential oil – peppermint and lavender are a good choice – to aid concentration. Before you start your studies, pause and think about what you've previously learned and what you hope to get from the session ahead.

A blessings book ritual

Intention: To spend time creating
a blessings book and rebuild connections
with the people in its pages.

This ritual is a lovely way to get creative once a week and to celebrate your connections with others at the same time. One of the best things we can do to benefit our emotional well-being is to nurture our relationships. Your blessings book will remind you of what makes your loved ones special and prompt you to contact them.

You could use:

- A large scrapbook
- Photos, letters, cards and keepsakes
- Any other crafting materials
- Writing paper and envelopes

Start by making your book. Think about all the people who are important to you – family members, friends and loved ones – and create a page (or several pages) in your book for each person or group. Stick in photos, quotes or anecdotes of your favourite times together.

You could aim to work on your project once a week. On busy weeks you may just have 15 minutes in the evening to stick in a picture or two, or to flick through your book and reminisce. If you have a little more time, get in touch with someone from your book, send them a photo of your work or ask them for a contribution. Even better, take the time to visit them and make more memories to include in your project.

Whatever you choose to do with your blessings book time, do it meaningfully and without distractions. Honouring your connections is a rewarding experience that will leave you feeling happy and grateful.

A ritual for knotting a bracelet

Intention: To weave bracelets instilled with intention.

Knotting is perfect for rituals where you want to put a little of your energy into your work: with every knot you tie, you imbue your creation with your intention. You can carry out knotting rituals with anything that can be tied, but making bracelets will give you something pretty and practical to wear.

You could use:

- Hemp, twine, thread or cord
- Approx. seven seed beads or some small charms that fit your intention

Take three lengths of twine (of about 19 inches long) and tie them together with a knot at one end, leaving a couple of inches above the knot to fasten it when finished. Plait your threads together until you have a braid that's 2–3 inches long.

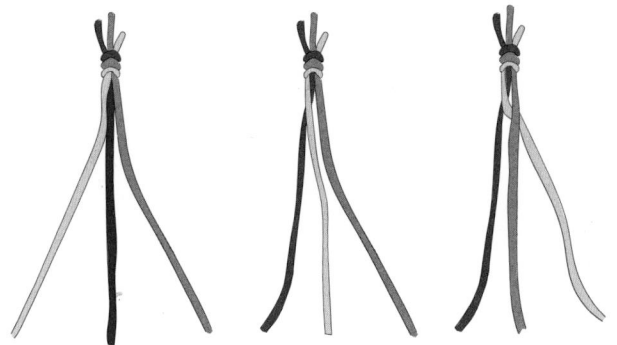

Once you have plaited 2–3 inches, add your first bead to the right-hand thread. Pull the right-hand thread over to the middle, making sure the bead is up snug beneath the braid. Then bring the left-hand thread into the centre. Add your second bead to the new right-hand thread and plait it to the centre. Then bring the left-hand thread to the centre. Continue adding beads from the right, then finish by braiding another 2–3-inch stretch and tying off.

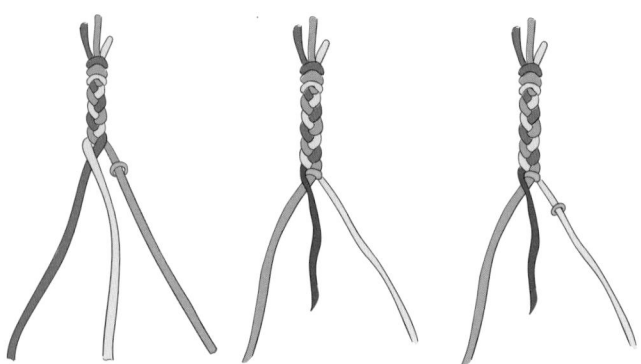

You could use seven coloured beads that correspond to the different chakras, binding in the attributes that each represents as you go. (Red for grounding; orange for creativity; yellow for power; green for love; blue for communication; indigo for psychic abilities and violet for spiritual connection.) Alternatively, use any charms that appeal to you.

This is a lovely activity to do in a group: you can pass the bracelets around so that everyone adds their energy to each one. If you enjoy this ritual, you can make many bracelets as gifts, or to donate to charity. There's no need to imbue every bracelet with intent, of course. You can simply relax and let your mind wander while braiding.

A photo-a-day ritual

This ritual encourages you to find positives in your day and to celebrate them by doing something creative – and since both creativity and gratitude boost your happiness levels, it's doubly beneficial.

Commemorate every day with a single photograph; something that captures a special, unique, quirky, funny or moving moment. You might decide to have a theme across each week, or simply to document your high points. You could get creative and take arty images or just snap a shot when you see a right-place-right-time composition. Look out for your photo opportunity as you enjoy your day and you will find yourself homing in on those things that make life special. You could print your pictures and put them in an album, or just set up a folder on your phone and flick through them every now and then to remind yourself of what's made your year special so far.

Love
Rituals

A love-affirmation ritual

Intention: To appreciate your special person and deepen your connection.

It's not always easy to tell our loved-ones how much they mean to us, but setting aside a little time for expressing your appreciation will enhance your connection and make you both feel happier. This ritual gives you a moment together to focus on one another and remind yourselves of what's important.

You could use:

- A rose-scented candle or ylang ylang essential oil
- A token of your esteem
- Your loved one

Carry out this ritual at the same time every week if possible. If you make it a regular event, you'll be able to plan ahead and prepare a little token or gift to make it extra special.

Find somewhere you won't be disturbed and turn off your phone or any other distractions. Light the candle and sit together, spending a few moments holding hands or simply sitting in silence before you begin. Then take it in turns to say something positive and appreciative to your special person – it can be as deep or as funny as you like, from "I love how you butter your toast" to "I really admire the way you stand up for what you believe in."

Now present them with your token. It doesn't need to be expensive: you might write a little rhyme, draw a cartoon of your loved one or just give them one of their favourite chocolates. Hopefully your special person will feel able to reciprocate.

Remember this can work for any special relationship, so whether you want to honour your partner, parent or pet – just be careful with the candle! – you can use this ritual to show your appreciation.

Seasonal rituals to share

Intention: To celebrate the turning
of the seasons with your tribe.

Seasonal rituals with your loved ones help you to tune in to the passing of the year, giving everyone a chance to reflect on the passing months and talk about their experiences and challenges. These get-togethers will nourish your mind, body and spirit. The most important thing you need is your loved ones, but you can include seasonal homemade dishes, natural decorations (pine cones in autumn or a vase of summer flowers, for example) and candles and incense if you like. After you've eaten together try one of the following activities:

Spring – Make a "tree" of loose twigs and branches, and put it in the centre of your table. Invite everyone to write their wishes on paper leaves and hang them on the tree.

Summer – Take your celebration outside to make the most of the longer days, pack a picnic and sing together. (Take along any percussion instruments you can find – drumming together is enormous fun.) An evening bonfire is a must.

Autumn – Pass a bowl of fallen leaves around the table; each person takes a leaf from the bowl and drops it on the floor, naming something they would like to discard from their life at the same time. (After your ritual, sweep up the leaves and compost them.)

Winter – Diffuse a few drops of frankincense essential oil to promote well-being, and light a large gold candle. Sit together in candlelight and give everyone a smaller white candle. Ask them to inscribe it with an inspirational word for the year ahead, and then take turns to light these candles – with each person saying aloud their wish – from the flame in the centre of the table. After a moment of reflection, you can extinguish the individual candles for people to take home and burn over the next few days.

A ritual for another

Intention: To dedicate a space to a
loved one and a moment to holding
them in your thoughts.

There are often times when we are thinking about those
we love and want to send them our blessings or prayers.
Whatever your beliefs, the act of holding someone in
your thoughts is a powerful one.

Clear a small area to use for this ritual and cleanse it by
burning sage (see p.84) or incense before setting it up. It
could be that you simply light a candle for your recipient,
but you might like to include a photo of them, a piece
of rose quartz to represent your loving thoughts and a
written intention or wish that you would like to focus on.
As with all the rituals in this book, you can personalize

this ritual to suit your purpose: if your ritual is for good health, pick bloodstone or aventurine crystals; for good luck you could choose carnelian or citrine. If crystals aren't your thing, you could add any charms or symbols that represent your feelings.

Every day, light the candle and start your ritual by sitting quietly and grounding yourself. Picture healing, comforting energy flowing into you from the earth, and then picture your chosen person, wherever they might be. Imagine a cord of this golden healing energy flowing from your heart to theirs. Focus on your intention – you may like to speak this aloud: "I send you healing and love," for example.

At the end of your ritual, allow the energy cord to gently disappear, but hold on to the image of your recipient safe in a bubble of healing light.

A pick-and-mix family gathering ritual

Intention: To customize your own family ritual and make get-togethers even more special.

Whether you see each other every day or once in a blue moon, introducing a ritual to your family gathering is fun and a brilliant bonding exercise. (It's a nice thing to do when you meet up with your friends, too.) By choosing an activity or tradition that everyone can participate in, you're creating precious moments when everyone's attention is focused on one another.

All families are different so design your own ritual, using any of the following elements that appeal to you – or any other ideas that come to mind – and enjoy sharing them at your next get-together. Your ritual is sure to become a new tradition that will strengthen your family bond and to which everyone will look forward.

A board game night – Take turns to choose an old favourite or try something new. No arguing about the rules!

Hot chocolate treat tray – Lay out everything you need for luxurious drinks and let everyone help themselves.

Read aloud – Story time isn't just for the little ones. It's lovely to share stories as adults, too. Take turns to read aloud to one another or tell each other an anecdote from your week – the more dramatic the telling, the better!

Share your intentions – Invite everyone to write down their intentions for the week and keep them in a jar. Review your progress together next time you meet.

A traditional meal – Most family gatherings centre around food, so cook your favourite family fare or order up a takeaway.

An after-dinner walk – A great time to share news (and walk off the favourite family fare!).

A group hug – Who doesn't love a hug?

Making a ritual of giving

Intention: To plan and give a gift every day.

The benefits of altruistic behaviour include higher self-esteem, a stronger sense of belonging and greater happiness all round, so make it a ritual to give a gift a day. Giving is about spreading positive energy, so the gift of a compliment, a smile or a thoughtful gesture can be just as rewarding as an item.

If you're stuck for inspiration, there are apps that you can download to suggest ideas for your good deed each day. People appreciate small handmade items, too – a bookmark or some home-baked brownies are thoughtful gifts that will be put to good use!

It's also a nice idea to keep a note in your journal of the good vibes you've passed on. Have fun coming up with creative ways to carry out your daily giving ritual, and enjoy making a difference to someone else's day as well as your own.

A ritual for celebrating your achievements

Intention: To recognize and commemorate your successes each week, however small.

It's important to celebrate the little things in life as well as the big milestones, so don't be shy about recognizing your achievements. Put up a whiteboard in your home and invite everyone to write down any successes they're proud of. It can be anything you like, from passing a test or handling a tricky negotiation at work to getting out of the door wearing a matching pair of socks!

Be sure to congratulate everyone on their achievements – or if you live alone, congratulate yourself with a nice big cup of tea or glass of wine! Record the story of your achievement in your journal or share it with your family and friends: a sign of true friendship is someone who gets excited about your sock successes, too!

A moving-moments ritual

Intention: To add an element of ritual to special gatherings and appreciate our loved ones.

A group ritual can make gatherings with our loved ones more special, particularly on the occasions when we want to draw on one another's support, love and wisdom. You might want to gather everyone together when a youngster is coming of age, to celebrate a happy family milestone or to remember someone who is no longer with you. Get together as a group; enjoy sharing stories, wisdom and memories at these moments; and practise this ritual to help you all pause and appreciate the strength and special gifts that everyone brings to the group.

Invite everyone to bring a favourite food to your gathering or make plans to cook something together. Sit and share your meal, and suggest a toast that marks the occasion. After you've set aside any distractions, light a candle and sit together, focusing your attention on one another.

Pass a feather around the circle and allow the person holding it to speak to each person in the group in turn, if they wish, saying something relevant to the occasion. It might be a simple message of happiness for someone's birthday or it may be to recount a favourite story or memory.

At the end of your get-together, give everyone a parting gift: have a supply of paper slips ready and invite everyone to write positive comments or compliments for one another on them. These can be as simple as "I love your dress sense" or as deep as "Your courage has always inspired me." You can make them anonymous if you wish: just leave the slips in a pile by each person's chair or pop them into their bag before they leave.

A loving-kindness ritual

Intention: To tune in to your compassionate side and transform your interactions with others.

It's very common for us to make judgements about the people we meet... and they may not be particularly flattering ones. Although we don't express these thoughts aloud, thinking them is still a negative process, so by learning to react to others from a place of kindness and compassion you'll be improving your mindset and the way you experience your day. Have a loving-kindness day: before you go out, tell yourself that you will see the light in everyone you meet, rather than focusing on the negatives (which may be caused by situations you don't understand).

Sit for a few moments and repeat the mantra "I am filled with loving kindness," then go out and spread some love and light. Make an effort to beam compassion and acceptance out to everyone you encounter and you will be surprised at how good it makes you feel, too.

You can also include a loving-kindness meditation at the end of your day. Sit quietly, ground yourself and imagine that you are filled with loving, compassionate energy from the life source. Begin by thinking of the people closest to you and send waves of compassion to each of them in turn. Next, move on to your friends and send them loving energy, then expand your circle out to colleagues and acquaintances. With practice you should be able to expand your energy meditation to make peace with those people you find it harder to get along with. This is very good spiritual practice!

A long-distance love ritual

Intention: To strengthen bonds and find comfort when you're spending time apart from a loved one.

This ritual can be a great source of comfort and strength when you have to spend time away from someone you care about. It helps you to set aside a time and place to think about your loved one and is a touchstone for you to tune in to your special connection.

You could use:

- A picture of you with your loved one
- Two shells, stones or crystals
- A pretty glass
- A small jug of water, charged under the full moon, if you like
- A pink or red candle inscribed with your initials

Choose a stone, crystal or shell to represent each of you. If you can choose these tokens for one another, that will make the ritual even more special. (Exchange your tokens and say a few words about why you picked your item, if you wish.) Set up a space to dedicate to your loved one while you are apart – you can do this part together or alone. Add your photo, candle and any other meaningful items. Put the glass in the centre of your space. Light the candle and spend a few moments quietly thinking about your special connection.

Now put the two tokens together in the glass and pour water over the top until they are submerged. (Water is the element of love and this ritual symbolizes a deep emotional connection.) When you're ready, extinguish the candle. While you are apart you can spend a few moments every day with the candle lit sending your special person loving thoughts. Keep the water topped up – but don't worry if you don't always have time to do it. (This is a blessing, not a love spell.) If you are to be apart for a while, you should refresh the water completely when necessary.

A ritual to help you nurture your relationships

Intention: To maintain the connections that gladden your heart.

The relationships we build with others are our primary source of happiness and help to define who we are. It can be easy to neglect these special connections in the flurry of yet another busy week, so make time to nurture them mindfully on a regular basis. This is something you could include in your evening "me time", if you like.

You could write a quick note to a friend you haven't seen in a while or send them a text, but if you're not a letter (or text) writer, your connections don't need to suffer. It's so easy to take a photo of something you see during the day to send with a quick caption, or to text them the cover of a book they might like, share a recipe or tweet with them, recommend a movie... anything that shows you're thinking of them. (Of course, if you can arrange a face-to-face meet-up, that's even better.)

Solo
Adventures

A ritual for embracing solitude

Intention: To enjoy your own company and indulge in some alone time.

Solitude often has negative connotations and is linked with the idea of loneliness, but spending time in our own company is actually essential for our well-being and can be a positive experience. We need these moments alone to connect with our thoughts and make sense of our interactions. Including them in our week will help us to combat stress and to maintain strong relationships in the time we do spend with others. It has even been shown to boost creativity, too.

This is a ritual that reminds you to embrace solitude and enjoy a little time alone. It's very simple. Each week plan a solitary outing and put it in your diary. (You could plan this at the weekend: look at the week ahead and choose what will work best for you.) You could even draw up a list of suitable trips or activities – things you've always wanted to do but haven't quite fitted in.

Plan ahead to make the most of your alone time: whether you spend it hiking, savouring a coffee in a quiet corner of your favourite cafe, watching a film or appreciating a different painting one lunchtime a week at a local gallery. Enjoy your own company, be at peace with your own thoughts and reflections, and look forward to treating yourself – you deserve it.

A make-a-date-with-the-moon ritual

Intention: To reflect each week with the moon as your guide and companion.

Many of us find that our emotional cycles tie in to the phases of the moon. The moon's transition – from new to full and back – provides a lovely framework for you to schedule in weekly rituals of self-reflection and self-care. Make a note of the moon's phases in your diary and pencil in rituals for the nights of the full and new moon – a fortnight apart. Add in a waxing-moon ritual (about seven days after your new moon date) and a waning-moon ritual (about seven days after the full moon).

You could start each ritual with a relaxing salt bath, then dress in something simple and free-flowing. If you're able to carry out your ritual beneath the moon, that's wonderful, but don't worry if not. You could meditate on images of the moon, hold a piece of moonstone or light white or silver candles to represent the moon in your ritual.

Use each moon date as a time to reflect back on your week and note in your journal how you're feeling, physically and emotionally. Are you feeling sensitive, inspired, happy or down? As you become familiar with how you feel across the month, you can adapt the rest of your ritual to suit. (Many people feel more sensitive at the new moon, for example, so they nurture themselves more around this time.)

New moon – A great time for fresh starts. You might like to perform a cleansing ritual or set intentions (see p.80).

Waxing – A good time for practical rituals, and to put in the work needed to achieve your goals. (You could perform a ritual for attracting prosperity – see p.94.)

Full moon – A time for manifestations and rewards. Assess your progress with projects, celebrate your achievements and indulge in something playful. (This is a good time to focus on your blessings book, for example – see p.118.)

Waning – Release anything unhelpful in your life. Ponder what's holding you back and perform any rituals for moving on and healing, such as the ritual on p.74.

Walking rituals

A walking ritual will give you all the benefits of being outside, but you can adapt your session to fit your emotional and spiritual needs for the day. Both these rituals will help if your mind is racing, but Ritual One is good for getting your thoughts in order, whereas Ritual Two will nourish the spirit and help you to reconnect with your surroundings.

Walking ritual one: The speedy walk

Intention: To clear your head and
organize your thoughts.

If your head is buzzing with thoughts, this is the ritual for you. Put on some comfortable shoes and take a brisk walk down a familiar route. Listen to music if you wish but pick a familiar playlist and keep the volume down so you can hear your train of thought. Walk as quickly as you can or jog, if you prefer. The main thing is to give your body something energetic and familiar to do. This will distract your "doing" mind enough to give your "thinking" mind the chance it needs to organize your thoughts. By the time you've reached the end of your route, you're sure to have a better perspective on things.

Walking ritual two: The s-l-o-w walk
Intention: To slow down, de-stress
and explore your environment.

If you're trying to introduce more mindfulness to your day, this ritual is an easy way to start. Head outside for a walk but take it slow and you'll start to notice more about the world around you. As we reduce our speed we give our minds the chance to absorb more information about our surroundings. Stop to look at the details of things: explore side streets, peer at the bark of a tree, read noticeboards and exchange smiles with the people you meet. Follow your instincts and, when you've finished your slow walk, you'll be calmer and happier for it.

A ritual to treat your senses

Intention: To enjoy the benefits of mindfulness and treat each of your senses in turn.

Mindfulness is all about engaging our senses and using them to experience the present moment fully, helping to anchor us in the here-and-now and avoid pondering the worries of the past and present. By selecting items that appeal to each of your different senses and including them in one ritual, you can indulge yourself and experience the benefits of mindfulness at the same time.

Choose whatever you like best. Here are some suggestions:

An aroma – freshly baked bread or freshly brewed coffee; a box of wax crayons; a room fragrance that evokes newly mown grass or a favourite scented candle.

A taste – salty anchovies; juicy olives; a fine wine; bitter dark chocolate or ripe berries.

A visual treat – a jaw-dropping photo of a natural wonder; a print of a favourite work of art; the colours of a sunset or a cherished family photo.

A sound – your favourite song or album; natural sounds such as breaking waves, raindrops or whale song; the sound of a crackling log fire or some meditative drumming.

Something tactile – stroke a pet; pop some bubble wrap; roll some modelling clay; snuggle yourself in silky pyjamas or a soft blanket or shell some pistachios (and eat them!).

Find somewhere comfortable and quiet to carry out your ritual and gather together your supplies. Concentrate on each in turn, remembering to focus fully on engaging your different senses and enjoying each element you choose. You could start by listening to your soundtrack, closing your eyes and concentrating on the melody or sounds; then turn your attention to savouring your snack and appreciating the flavours, for example. Exactly how you complete your ritual is up to you – and you can choose different combinations of experiences every time, if you like.

A lunchtime ritual

Intention: To establish and enjoy
the benefits of a good lunchtime ritual.

Whatever you do for a living, chances are your day is packed with commitments from start to finish. Multi-tasking and rushing from one thing to the next can be very draining, so taking a proper break at lunchtime is essential and will improve your productivity in the afternoon.

Lunchtime is *your* time, so embrace it and make sure it works for you. The best lunchtime ritual you can develop will include the following:

Lunch! – eating a sandwich with one hand while checking emails with the other is not a lunch break! Be sure to take time away from your desk to eat your lunch and to focus on your food.

Time outside – getting some fresh air during the day boosts your mood and your health, so even if it's just a quick walk around the block, make time for it if you can.

A chat – turn off your devices and talk to someone face to face – whether you get to know a colleague or meet up with a friend for a quick catch-up. A non-work-related chat is a great break for the brain.

A change of scene – if you can, make the most of your time and plan a visit to a local gallery, museum or somewhere scenic to sit with a book. Safeguard and savour your "me" time.

A moment of self-care – practise a quick meditation or some breathwork and you'll feel calmer and happier in the afternoon.

A new intention – before you tackle your afternoon to-do list, take a moment to pause and set an intention for the afternoon ahead.

A ritual for spiritual journeying

Intention: To explore your unconscious mind and find comfort there.

For this adventure you don't even need to leave your home: all you need is your imagination. This is a nice visualization to do before you sleep as you can adapt it to suit your mood. Turn off any distractions and settle down as you would to meditate. Lying down is fine as it's okay to drift off during your journey; this can lead to interesting and healing dreams. Relax your body and focus on your breathing.

Start by visualizing your ideal sanctuary. This may be an existing place or somewhere imaginary. Perhaps it's a cosy bedroom, a luxury yacht or a tree house in the forest. Picture all the details of your environment and imagine yourself sitting comfortably in your special place. You feel peaceful and serene.

Now imagine you're leaving your haven and setting off on a journey through the landscape outside. Your destination will depend on how you feel today. If you're in search of peace, you may walk to a deserted beach and lie on the sand with crystal-clear water lapping at your toes; if you're in need of spiritual healing, walk into the forest and sit within the hollow trunk of an ancient oak; if you need to feel grounded, visit an ancient stone circle and lie back against a sun-warmed stone.

If you need advice, invite other figures to join you: for wisdom, find a guru by the campfire; for healing, seek a shaman in the forest; and for inspiration ask for a gift from whoever you meet. (The symbolism of what you're given is worth thinking about later.)

Every time you repeat this ritual, you will add details to your imaginary landscape that will reflect your needs. Your starting point may be the same, but you are free to make different journeys whenever you wish – just let your imagination guide you, and enjoy.

Conclusion

I hope this book has shown you how simple and rewarding it can be to include rituals in your everyday life, and that it has inspired you to experiment with them. Remember, you don't need to follow the suggestions in this book to the letter — customizing the rituals will make them more personal to you and is part of the fun. You may even feel inspired to create some rituals of your own.

If you're new to rituals, why not try something easy to start with, such as a bathing ritual, or adding a ritual element to your morning or evening routine. Think about the more stressful parts of your day and see whether you can improve them with a ritual or two. (There's always something you can do to bring a little calm and positivity to these challenging moments.)

However you choose to include rituals in your life, remember that they are wonderful tools for enhancing your day but should never become a nuisance. If a particular ritual doesn't work for you, that's fine. There's no need to persevere with it when there are so many other ideas you can try. And don't feel bad if you can't always carry out a ritual when planned; there will always be another opportunity to give it a go.

Above all, enjoy discovering the brilliant benefits that rituals can offer you. I hope that you find time to treat yourself to some of these precious moments of calm and to experience a little peace and positivity every day.

List of Rituals

If you're interested in finding out more about
our books, find us on Facebook at
Summersdale Publishers and follow us
on Twitter at @Summersdale.

www.summersdale.com